Creative Times

with God

Doug Fields

Illustrations by Steve Bjorkman

HARVEST HOUSE PUBLISHERS
Eugene, Oregon 97402

CREATIVE TIMES WITH GOD

Copyright © 1988 by Harvest House Publishers
Eugene, Oregon 97402

Library of Congress Catalog Card Number 87-081665
ISBN 0-89081-618-2

Printed in the United States of America.

To Todd Temple,
whose love for life and consistent friendship
have ignited my creativity
and inspired my love for God.

Special thanks to Scott Rachels,
whose creativity, enthusiasm, and humor
have brought great joy to my life.

Contents

INTRODUCTION

I thought I'd made a big mistake when I asked some members of my youth group what they thought about the Bible.

"The Bible is boring. Let's go out for pizza."

"It's too hard to understand."

"Why do I have to read it every day at the same time?"

After hearing these negative responses, I asked them what we could do to make the Bible a more significant and positive part of our Christian growth.

Creative Times with God is one of the results of our discussion.

Many of us enter into a relationship with God with a burning desire to understand the Bible. We eagerly want to study it, memorize it, and live it. In our early enthusiasm, we seek guidance for personal Bible study. We're directed to begin a daily "quiet time" at the same hour of the day, using the same materials in the same way every day. We are loaded down with formats, structures, guidelines, charts, and expectations. And in our excitement we dive in and do it—we'll try anything!

But as time passes we get tired of the monotonous routine. We start to lose interest. Our Bibles begin to collect dust and we feel guilty for missing our spiritual appointment with God.

We know that God desires for us to spend time with Him. If some of us can do it the same way at the same time every day—that's great. But some of us need variety and creativity to keep our devotional time fresh and alive. And that's great too—as long as we are spending time with God.

Creative Times with God was designed to introduce a spark of life to your times with God. I hope the devotional adventures in this book will ignite your creativity and fire up your passion for knowing God in a more personal and intimate manner.

May you grow and have fun!

—Doug Fields
Newport Beach, California

Creative Times with God

with God

Building an Adventurous Faith

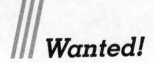

Wanted!

Imagine that you live in a country where Christianity is illegal. You are wanted for questioning by governmental authorities because you love and believe in God.

Place a photo or sketch of yourself in the "WANTED" poster below and enter your name beneath it. Then write a statement explaining what you believe—the reason you are wanted. If you need some help, see Matthew 16:13-16 and 1 Corinthians 15:1-5.

WANTED
FOR BELIEVING IN GOD

_____

(your name)

This suspect believes . . .

/// Self Serve

Prepare a menu of qualities which you feel are important for Christians to apply to their lives. Read Galatians 5:22-24 to help you think of specific qualities.

APPETIZERS: List qualities that are important for the beginning Christian.

1.

2.

3.

4.

SALAD BAR: List a variety of qualities that you would like to see in your life. Rank them in order of importance with number 1 being the most needed right now.

1.

2.

3.

4.

5.

6.

7.

8.

9.

10.

MAIN DISH: List some specific things you can do this month that will help you make your number 1 priority (listed on the preceding page) more attainable.

1.

2.

3.

4.

5.

6.

7.

DESSERT: Thank God for His greatness. Ask Him to help as you pursue your "main dish." Remember, God wants you to become more like His Son and He will help you in your pursuit of godliness.

God Is Like . . .

Look around the room and locate an object. Write the name of the object in the two spaces below. List in the left column some descriptive qualities of the object. Next to each quality in the right column write how you think God is similar (see the example, "God is like a shoe," below). If possible, find a verse which supports your description.

There are no right or wrong answers in this exercise. Write down whatever comes to mind. Make sure you take time to thank God for all the special blessings He brings into your life.

God is like a _____
(object)

_____   **God**
(object)

1.   1.

2.   2.

3.   3.

4.   4.

5.   5.

God is like a shoe

Shoe   **God**

1. Protects my feet   1. God protects me
(Psalm 91:2)

2. Helps me walk

2. God guides my path and helps me walk in the right direction (Psalm 119:105)

3. Dependable

3. God promises never to leave me (Matthew 28:20)

4. Come in pairs

4. I am not alone, God gave me His Holy Spirit to always be with me (John 14:16)

5. Many different styles

5. God loves all kinds of different people (Acts 10:34,35)

Next, try some of these: Jesus is like . . . , My church is like . . . , Heaven will be like . . . , God's love is like . . .

Alien Questions

For years people have speculated about life on other planets or galaxies. Imagine that an alien came to earth and asked you the following three questions. How would you respond?

1. What things do you like most about your life on planet earth?

2. What are the four most important things in your life right now?
   A.
   B.
   C.
   D.

3. What is so special about your Creator?

End your time by reading Ecclesiastes 12:1 and asking God to make you the person that He wants you to be.

Who Accepts Me?

Read the quote below and answer the questions which follow:

> I am afraid to tell you who I am, because, if I tell you who I am, you may not like who I am, and it's all that I have (John Powell, *Why Am I Afraid to Love?*).

1. Do you sometimes feel that if you opened up to someone they wouldn't accept you anymore? If so, why?

2. What scares you the most about telling others about your real self?

3. Do you think God accepts you no matter what your problems may be? If so, why? If not, why not?

4. Why is human acceptance so different from God's acceptance?

5. What can you do this week to be more accepting of others?

6. Read James 5:16 and comment on why James feels it is important for us to confess our sins to one another.

REMEMBER: GOD ACCEPTS YOU NOT FOR WHAT YOU DO (like your friends might) **BUT FOR WHO YOU ARE.**

Yes, I'm Positive

All of us crave positive comments from others, but we live in a society which seems to focus on the negative. We love to hear words such as "great job," but so often we only hear, "Why didn't you clean up your room?"

Read Matthew 12:33-37 to learn what Jesus had to say about the words we use. Then, in the spaces below, write three sincere, positive comments to five different people in your life (parents, teachers, coaches, youth minister, friends, sister, brother, neighbor, mailman, etc.).

After writing, say a prayer of thankfulness for each person. Then copy each message on a separate sheet of paper and deliver it to the appropriate person.

Here's an example of positive comments:

MOM

Thank you for always caring about me even though at times I don't act like I care about you.

You do a great job of making my friends feel comfortable when they come to our house.

You made me feel good the other day when you didn't yell at me for not completing my English assignment. Thanks for being understanding.

Person #1: _____

Person #2: _____

Person #3: _____

Person #4: _____

Person #5: _____

Love Notes

In 1 Corinthians 13:1-13 you will find a thorough description of love. Read the chapter and list below the qualities of love you find. Then evaluate the presence of that quality in your life by circling a number between 1 and 10 (1 means it is never present, 10 means it is always present, etc.). Next, write a brief note for each quality describing how you can improve the rating of this quality in your life.

QUALITY	NEVER		SOMETIMES					ALWAYS		

————————— 1 2 3 4 5 6 7 8 9 10

————————— 1 2 3 4 5 6 7 8 9 10

————————— 1 2 3 4 5 6 7 8 9 10

————————— 1 2 3 4 5 6 7 8 9 10

————————— 1 2 3 4 5 6 7 8 9 10

————————— 1 2 3 4 5 6 7 8 9 10

————————— 1 2 3 4 5 6 7 8 9 10

————————— 1 2 3 4 5 6 7 8 9 10

QUALITY	NEVER				SOMETIMES				ALWAYS	
_____	1	2	3	4	5	6	7	8	9	10
_____	1	2	3	4	5	6	7	8	9	10
_____	1	2	3	4	5	6	7	8	9	10
_____	1	2	3	4	5	6	7	8	9	10
_____	1	2	3	4	5	6	7	8	9	10
_____	1	2	3	4	5	6	7	8	9	10

Growing Strong

"I can do everything God asks me to with the help of Christ who gives me the strength and power" (Philippians 4:13 TLB).

List your five greatest achievements:

1.

2.

3.

4.

5.

List your five greatest strengths:

1.

2.

3.

4.

5.

What specific things keep you from building on these strengths?

Powerfully Weak

"Three different times I begged God to make me well again. Each time he said, 'No, But I am with you; that is all you need. My power shows up best in weak people.' Now I am glad to boast about how weak I am; I am glad to be a living demonstration of Christ's power, instead of showing off my own power and abilities. . . . For when I am weak, then I am strong—the less I have, the more I depend on him" (2 Corinthians 12:8-10 TLB).

Underline one phrase above which is most meaningful to you today. What is so special about this verse for you?

How does this Scripture passage relate to the things you listed in the last lesson which keep you from building on your strengths?

Write your own honest statement about your weaknesses. Conclude your statement with a prayer describing the growth you would like to see based on the verses above.

I'll write down my weaknesses for me and God,... but I'm not going to let you see them!

Gimme Five

Prayer is an important discipline in our walk with God. The Bible shows us many different ways by which we should communicate with God in prayer. Look up the verses in the left column and match them with the different kinds of prayer described in the right column. Then include all five kinds in your prayer time with God.

1. 1 Thessalonians 5:17   **THANKSGIVING:** Giving thanks to God for His work in our lives.

2. Ephesians 5:20   **SUPPLICATION:** Asking God to fill our need for something; making a request of God.

3. Philippians 4:6   **PRAISE:** Telling God how great and good He is; appreciating Him for who He is.

4. 1 John 1:9   **CONFESSION:** Stating our sins and failures openly to God in order to receive forgiveness.

5. Psalm 34:3, 150:2   **CONVERSATION:** Communicating with God naturally and continually.

One of Your Favorites

Write your favorite verse on a small piece of paper. (If you don't have a favorite, use a verse from a previous session.) Place the verse where you will see it and think about it through the day (in your notebook, in your shoe, on your steering wheel, etc.).

Read your verse often and pray, "Lord, what do You want me to learn from this verse today?" Before you go to bed, write down what God taught you and how it might relate to your life in the days ahead.

Today's Verse:

What God Taught Me About This Verse:

Blind Insight

Before you read today's Bible passage, try this
experiment. Perform one of your regular daily
activities either blindfolded or with your eyes closed
(for example, getting dressed, eating breakfast, or
making your bed). Simulate the experience of total
blindness for several minutes.

Then read how Jesus healed the blind man in Mark
8:22-26. After reading, look through a newspaper or
magazine until you find a picture of someone
suffering from blindness or another physical
limitation (for example, someone on a stretcher,
someone in a wheelchair, or an elderly person). Cut
out the picture and mount it in the space below.

What could you do today to minister to someone in need like Jesus ministered to the blind man? You may want to write an encouraging letter to someone, visit someone in the hospital, or take cookies to an invalid in a nursing home. Decide on one ministry activity and carry it out.

After completing your task, thank God for your physical sight and health and ask Him to increase your sensitivity to needy people. Consider what you and/or your youth group can do on a regular basis to help meet the needs of the blind, elderly, or handicapped in your community.

Where's the Match?

Look up the verses in the left column and draw a line from each to its corresponding meaning in the right column. Read carefully and think about the entire verse or passage.

Matthew 7:1-5   Confess your sins to one
                                 another

Romans 6:6-11   God's unconditional love

John 3:16   Christ now lives in me

James 5:16   Being spiritually mediocre

Revelation 3:16   Jesus died for our sins

Galatians 2:20   Check out your own life
                                 before you judge

Bank on It

A Christian banker tells you he sees a lot of comparisons between his bank and the church. "For example," he says, "with the help of the automatic teller machines the bank doesn't need to be open for people to get what they want. In the same way, the church building doesn't need to be open for people to talk to God."

What are some more similarities you can think of between the church and the following features of a bank? Add a few of your own which come to mind.

1. The building

2. The money

3. The personnel or staff

4. The vault

5. Interest and/or interest rates

6. The service

7.

8.

9.

Before you finish, read Acts 2:42-47. Thank God for the church you attend and ask Him to bless its leadership.

Sunday Morning Circus

Everyone loves the circus! What if the church resembled a circus and church leaders took the roles of circus characters? What kind of church would we have?

Complete the list of circus characters on the left. Then describe the kinds of pastoral qualities each character might contribute to the church from their circus experience. Read 1 Timothy 3:1-13 and Titus 1:6-9 for some biblical qualities for church leaders.

Circus Characters	Pastoral Qualities
1. Ringmaster	1.
2. Clown	2.
3. Tightrope walker	3.
4. Lion tamer	4.
5. Juggler	5.
6. Make-up artist	6.
7.	7.
8.	8.
9.	9.
10.	10.

Fishing Your Crowd

Jesus knew what kind of language to use to reach a particular audience. When He was looking for disciples He came upon some fishermen. His invitation to follow was spoken in terms they understood. " 'Come, follow me,' Jesus said, 'and I will make you fishers of men.' At once they left their nets and followed him" (Mark 1:17,18 NIV).

How would you describe the type of audience you have the opportunity to reach?

What kind of "language" do you need to speak in order to reach them?

What specific things do you need to do in order to reach them?

Identify by name the group that you will attempt to reach for Christ this week.

I Am

In the Gospel of John, Jesus used seven "I am" statements to describe Himself and His ministry. Read these "I am" statements and write down what you think Jesus meant by each of them.

1. John 6:35,41,48,51   I am the _____.

2. John 8:12; 9:5   I am the _____.

3. John 10:7,9   I am the _____

4. John 10:11,14   I am the _____

5. John 11:25   I am the _____

6. John 14:6   I am the _____

7. John 15:1,5   I am the _____

If Jesus were on the earth today, what kind of "I am" statement might He use to describe Himself so that we could better understand Him? Why?

I am the _____

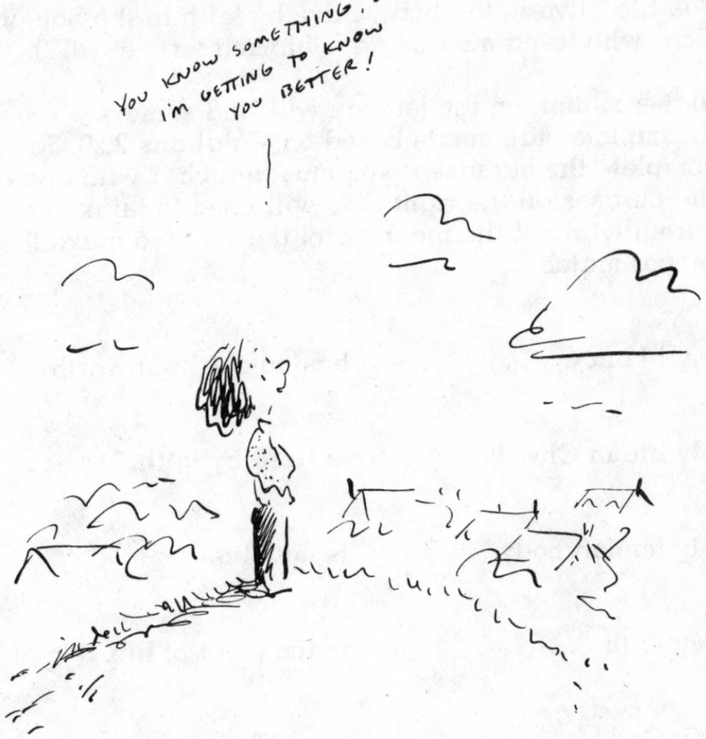
YOU KNOW SOMETHING, LORD?
I'M GETTING TO KNOW
YOU BETTER!

Dead but Alive

Galatians 2:20 reads, "I have been crucified with Christ and I no longer live, but Christ lives in me. The life I live in the body, I live by faith in the Son of God, who loved me and gave himself for me" (NIV).

In the column on the left you will find some incomplete statements based on Galatians 2:20. To complete the statement you must match it with one of the phrases on the right. You will need to think carefully about the meaning of the verse to make the proper match.

My life now . . .   has no spiritual worth.

My life in Christ . . .   is lived by faith.

My human body . . .   is new life.

My faith . . .   is the giver of life.

My God . . .   is in Christ.

Take time to thank God in writing for His loving sacrifice. Ask God for guidance in your life of faith.

Putting the Romans Together

The four sentences below are from Romans 5:20,21 (TLB), but they are listed in incorrect order. Read each sentence carefully and see if you can figure out the correct order, numbering them accordingly. As you think about the correct order, jot down what each sentence is saying to you. Then check your answer to the puzzle by looking up Romans 5:20,21.

_____ "But the more we see our sinfulness, the more we see God's abounding grace forgiving us."

_____ "The Ten Commandments were given so that all could see the extent of their failure to obey God's laws."

_____ "Resulting in eternal life through Jesus Christ our Lord."

_____ "Before, sin ruled over all men and brought them to death, but now God's kindness rules instead, giving us right standing with God."

The Winning Team!

The Body of Christ (all Christians) can be compared
to an athletic team which works together to win.
Read Romans 12:3-8 and 1 Corinthians 12:12-26 to see
the description of how the Body of Christ should work
together. As you read, list below the similarities
between the Body of Christ and an athletic team (see
the two examples). Be sure to include a Scripture
reference to support your similarities.

Athletic Team	Body of Christ	Scripture
1. Everyone is talented	God gives gifts to us all	Romans 12:4
2. Players have different positions	Christians have different gifts	Romans 12:6
3.		
4.		
5.		

6.

7.

8.

9.

10.

Living It Up

Take a few minutes to read John 3:1-36. As you read, notice that there seems to be three types of life mentioned: physical life, spiritual life, and eternal life. Answer the following questions as you work through the passage.

When does each type of life begin?

Physical

Spiritual

Eternal

What do you see as significant about each type of life?

Physical

Spiritual

Eternal

How are the three types of life related to each other?

Physical

Spiritual

Eternal

How can you use what you have learned in this chapter to help others in the years to come?

A Friend(ly) Job Description

A job description specifies the expectations a boss holds for an employee. Job descriptions often explain in detail how employees should behave, dress, and work.

Read Proverbs 16:7; 17:9,17; 18:24; and 27:6,9. Then write a job description of a good friend based on these verses. Include specific qualities which outline how a friend should behave.

A Good Friend Should . . .

According to this job description, are you a good friend? Why or why not?

What could you do this week to improve as a good friend?

Shopping Spree

Welcome to an imaginary store that sells only qualities, skills, and spiritual gifts. You have $100 to spend on whatever you want. Shop wisely because you can never come back to this store again. Circle the items you will buy which total no more than $100. Then answer the questions on the next page.

Items for Sale

$ 90	athletic talent	$ 45	forgiveness
$ 35	encouragement	$ 30	self-control
$ 75	singing skills	$ 60	faith
$101	eternal life	$ 65	peace
$ 40	wisdom	$ 25	writing skills
$ 50	acting ability	$ 40	speaking in tongues
$ 30	patience	$ 20	stress management
$ 65	future knowledge	$ 30	leadership
$ 25	gentleness	$ 20	joy
$ 35	communication skills	$ 45	servanthood
$ 45	organization	$ 85	ability to heal
$ 70	humility	$ 25	sensitivity
$ 40	sense of humor	$ 35	hope

Why did you select the items you circled?

How are your "purchases" going to change your life in the future?

Would God choose the same items for you? Why or why not?

How do your selections compare to the list of qualities in Philippians 4:8?

My Significant Other

As Paul worked to spread the Gospel and establish churches he apparently enjoyed several significant relationships. Timothy was one young man Paul spent time with and trained. Paul called Timothy his "true son in the faith" (1 Timothy 1:2 NIV). The New Testament letters bearing Timothy's name were written by Paul to encourage him, instruct him, and advise him. Timothy counted on Paul's maturity and wisdom to help him grow and lead others.

Is there an older, wiser, and more mature Christian in your life who could be a "Paul" to you? Is there a younger Christian in your life who might be a "Timothy" to you? Identify these people below.

List some people you might like to be your "Paul":

List some people you think could become your "Timothy":

List at least five important qualities which should be found in someone who takes the role of a "Paul" Christian to a "Timothy" Christian:

Pardoned from Jail

Read the verses on the topic of forgiveness which are listed below. Then write a letter to a fictitious prisoner who is locked up on a murder charge. The prisoner doesn't believe that God will forgive him even though he has accepted Christ as his Lord. The purpose of your letter is to convince him of God's forgiveness. Support your position with Scripture.

1 John 1:9; Ephesians 4:32; Mark 3:28-30; Romans 4:7,8

Your Serve

Jesus came to earth as a servant and desired to leave His mark of servanthood on this world. Mark 10:45 reads, "For even the Son of Man did not come to be served, but to serve, and to give his life a ransom for many" (NIV).

Read John 13:1-20. Jesus chose this form of service to communicate servanthood to His disciples. What are some creative ways you can serve the significant people in your life *today* (for example, washing the dishes without being told, conserving hot water for your brother or sister's shower)? List your decisions for service below.

How are you going to serve these people today?

Parents:

Brothers/sisters:

Friends:

Neighbors:

Teachers:

Boss:

Heavy Weight

In Psalm 38, David pleads for God's mercy in his troubles and seeks God's deliverance from all his wrongful acts. In verse 4 he says, "My guilt has overwhelmed me like a burden too heavy to bear" (NIV).

In an attempt to understand what David meant in this verse, try something very different. Take a large pillowcase and fill it with books (textbooks, encyclopedia, etc.). Then carry the filled pillowcase during your daily chores and activities. It will be difficult and frustrating, but what you learn will make the struggle worthwhile.

After completing the exercise, answer the following questions:

How are your sins weighing you down?

What three sins do you consistently struggle with?

Ask God in writing to forgive your sins, to help you in your pursuit of Him, and to teach you a lasting lesson through your exercise.

Brand Name

Look through a magazine to find an advertisement which is seemingly unrelated to the product it is trying to sell (for example, an ad for deodorant showing a businessman at the top of his profession, apparently because he uses a certain deodorant).

Advertisers appeal to our emotions hoping to provoke a favorable response for their product. Often the emotional appeal has little or nothing to do with the product. This subtle form of manipulation hopes to build within us a craving for brand names which will make us feel popular, powerful, or prestigious.

Read Romans 12:3. Then in the space below create a brand name and a label design which correctly describes you. (For example, a brand name could be Uniquecre—a composite of unique and creative— representing a desire to be different from the norm and creative in living.) Then explain why you chose your brand name and design.

Pray Your Cards Right

Jesus said, "When you pray, go into your room, close the door and pray to your Father, who is unseen. Then your Father, who sees what is done in secret, will reward you" (Matthew 6:6 NIV).

Take a deck of playing cards into your prayer time today. Shuffle the deck and begin to lay the cards face up one-by-one until you have turned over four of a kind. With each card you turn, offer a sentence prayer following this pattern:

When you turn over a **heart** say a prayer of thankfulness.

When you turn over a **spade** ask for forgiveness in an area of your life.

When you turn over a **diamond** pray for your dreams, goals, and future.

When you turn over a **club** pray for your family, your youth group, or another organization you belong to.

THANKS FOR THE GIFT OF LAUGHTER!

Grand Entrance

Sin separated mankind from God. In order to bridge the sin gap, God chose to send His only Son, Jesus Christ, to the earth so that we might be reunited with God.

If you were the God of the universe, how would you have chosen for your Son Jesus to make His entrance into the world (for example, out of the sky during the middle of the Super Bowl)?

Read Matthew 1:18-25 and Luke 2:1-20 to discover how Jesus did enter our world. How would you summarize Jesus' entrance?

Why do you think God chose for Jesus to come into the world the way He did?

Reporting the News

Imagine that you are a news journalist covering the event of Jesus' triumphal entry into Jerusalem. Your story may be broadcast on the six o'clock news or hit the front page of the Jerusalem Daily Pilot.

Read the facts in Matthew 21:1-22 and pretend that you are on the scene. As you write your story be sure to include Jesus' activities at the Temple, the significance of the fig tree, and the reaction of the crowd. Hope to see you on the news!

Thanks for Me

Psalm 139 explains that God sees everywhere and knows everything about us. Verses 13-16 describe that God even knew us before we were born.

Read the entire psalm, paying special attention to verses 13-16. Then write a letter to God thanking Him for His greatness. Include your gratitude for His creative design in making you. Ask God to forgive you for complaining about how you were created.

Dear God,

DEAR GOD—
THANKS FOR MAKING ME
A LIZARD. I KNOW I
COMPLAIN SOMETIMES
ABOUT THE SCALES,
BUT ALL IN ALL I
LIKE THE FACT THAT
I HAVE A FORKED
TONGUE AND MY
TAIL CAN GROW BACK.

A Word from the Sponsor

Below on the left is a list of five "channels" representing different elements of the Christian faith. On the right are five different "commercials" (verses) which belong to the five channels. Read each of the commercial references and match them with the correct channels.

Channels	Commercials
Forgiveness	1 Corinthians 12:4-6
Salvation	1 John 1:9
Eternal Life	John 3:3-8
Spiritual Gifts	Acts 1:8
Witnessing	John 3:36

Very Tempting

Read Luke 4:1-13, the description of the temptations Jesus faced in the desert. Then complete the following exercises.

Look up the word "temptation" in the dictionary and write the definition in your own words.

List five temptations which give you the greatest difficulty (for example: money, popularity, sex, cheating).

1.

2.

3.

4.

5.

Write out 1 Corinthians 10:13. How does this verse give you hope for the temptations you face?

Thank God that He knows all the temptations and feelings we experience.

Money Matters

Jesus talked a lot about money and wealth—and sometimes we pretend not to hear Him. Read what He said about wealth in Luke 12:13-21.

List ten things you own which give you the greatest satisfaction.

1.

2.

3.

4.

5.

6.

7.

8.

9.

10.

Then write beside each item what you think it will mean to you ten years from now.

Ask God to help you make the right decisions with your money and possessions because "every man is a fool who gets rich on earth but not in heaven" (Luke 12:21 TLB).

No Worries

In the previous lesson you read about riches in Luke 12:13-21. Following this section, Jesus talked to His disciples about worrying (a problem that many of us have). Read what Jesus said about worrying in Luke 12:22-31.

Go outside and find a flower, a leaf, or blade of grass to keep with you until tomorrow. Every time you look at it or feel it in your pocket, say a quick prayer of thanksgiving for God's provision for you.

If you need to be more thankful during your week, remember the lilies and rejoice that "your heavenly Father knows your needs" (Luke 12:30 TLB).

Table Talk

Move to the kitchen table or dining room table to complete this exercise. Think of five items which are often on the table you're sitting at (for example: knife, napkin, saltshaker). List them in the column on the left.

Then think of a verse or spiritual truth that each object suggests to you. For example, a knife may suggest Hebrews 4:12: "The word of God is living and active. Sharper than any double-edged sword. . . ." (NIV). Or a napkin may remind you that God wipes away our sin when we ask His forgiveness. Jot your ideas in the column on the right.

Each time you use these items at the table this week, thank God for the truth they represent.

Table Object	Truth It Represents
1.	1.
2.	2.
3.	3.
4.	4.
5.	5.

Lame Excuses

Read John 5:1-13. Notice the excuse the invalid used in verse seven to defend his disability. If this story happened today, what kinds of excuses might the invalid use to explain why he hadn't taken advantage of God's provisions? List five possible excuses below (be creative and humorous if you like).

Excuses

1.

2.

3.

4.

5.

Now write down the names of three people you know who are making lame excuses for their relationships with God. Take time to pray for each of them asking God to heal them like He healed the invalid at the pool.

People

1.

2.

3.

I REALLY WOULD LIKE TO ASK GOD FOR HEALING, BUT I THOUGHT I SHOULD WAIT 'TIL CHRISTMAS WHEN HE'S FEELING GENEROUS.

Now that you have thought about others, are you using any lame excuses which you need to confess to God as you seek His healing?

Prayer Pattern

In Matthew 6:9-13 Jesus gave His disciples an example of prayer in what we often call the Lord's prayer. He didn't say, "Always pray these words," but rather He suggested, "Pray along these lines" (Matthew 6:9 TLB). Look at the Lord's prayer as a *style* of praying instead of a required prayer which must be recited the same way each time.

Below are the phrases of the Lord's prayer from the familiar King James' Version. Pray through each phrase by making it personal to you.

"Our Father which art in heaven, hallowed be thy name."
Spend some time praising and thanking God for His fatherly characteristics and His holy name.

"Thy kingdom come. Thy will be done in earth, as it is in heaven."
Now is a good time to pray for God's will to be done in yourself and in the lives of your family and friends.

"Give us this day our daily bread."
Pray now that God would feed you spiritually as you read His Word.

"And forgive us our debts, as we forgive our debtors."
Ask God for personal forgiveness. Then ask Him to remind you of people you need to forgive.

"And lead us not into temptation, but deliver us from evil."
Pray now for God to protect you from things that tempt you.

"For thine is the kingdom, and the power, and the glory, forever. Amen."
Conclude your prayer as you began it—with praise to God for His greatness.

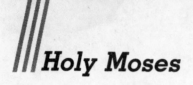

Holy Moses

Moses was a man God used in mighty ways to lead Israel out of captivity and into the Promised Land. Read Exodus 3:1—4:17 to discover how God called Moses to his task. Then answer the questions below.

How do you think God would most like to use you?

What great mission would you like to embark on for God? Describe in detail what you would like to do for God. Then write a prayer asking God to start preparing you to do His work in His time.

Missionary Journey

The book of Acts reveals how the early church was born and grew. Paul and others traveled to different cities to preach the gospel, help believers, and plant churches. We refer to Paul's travels as missionary journeys. Read Acts 13:2,3 to see how Paul's missionary journeys began.

Get a map of your community and highlight the areas you would visit if God called you to take a missionary journey. Spend some time in prayer for each of the areas you have highlighted. Then answer the following questions.

What would be your strategy to reach each of these areas?

What is the possibility that you could actually do something like this in your community?

Who would you want to take with you? Why?

What kind of person do you think God would call to do something like this? What needs to happen to make you this kind of person?

Straight and Narrow

Your youth group wants to start a Bible club on campus next semester and they have asked you to provide the leadership. But during final exams, a week before the new semester begins, you discover that your grades may not be good enough for you to serve as the school representative for a campus club. After figuring your GPA you discover that you need A's on your last two finals. Your best grades so far have been C's.

You don't want to disappoint your youth group, but you know you'll never be a club rep next semester . . . unless you cheat on those last two exams. You sit next to A students in both classes and you know you can pull it off without getting caught. What will you do?

Read the following verses to see how they might help you in this confusing situation: Exodus 20:15; Proverbs 10:2; 12:5; 14:2; 15:16; Romans 7:18-25; Galatians 6:7; 1 Thessalonians 4:6; 1 John 2:6.

Write an honest letter to your youth group explaining your situation and describing what you have learned from God's Word. State what you are going to do based on your convictions. Also include your advice to others who may be facing similar situations.

Dear Youth Group,

Train Stop

Read Galatians 6:10. Then imagine that you have access to four trains. Each train is loaded with one of the following qualities and ready to distribute them at your direction:

Honesty   Godliness   Laughter   Security

You happen to know about four cities which are having problems. Each city needs one of the above trains to remedy their situation. Read each description below and decide which of the four trains should be sent there. Write your decision beneath each description and explain the reason for your selection.

City #1

This city has gone downhill ever since the new mayor was elected. He is trying to pass laws that will make his office and staff look good. But his laws are doing nothing for the good of the city. People are angry but they lack the power to pressure the mayor to change.

City #2

The people in City #2 don't know what to do about all the stealing that is going on in their community. Homes are being burglarized, schools are being vandalized, and stores are going out of business because of robbery and theft. The police department is too small to stop all the crime.

City #3

No one seems to care in this city. There is no public participation in any activities. The churches are empty, the parks are deserted, and no one attends civic planning meetings. Kids don't play after school, neighbors don't talk to each other, and everyone is chained to his or her work.

City #4

People have been living in this city for many years. Families are strong and community relationships are good. But unemployment is a serious problem. Some people must travel over 100 miles each way to work. And those who do work in the city earn very little because of the depressed economy.

Hidden Sins

Each word in **bold** print in the following verses can also be found in the word search puzzle below. See if you can find all the words in under five minutes.

"You were dead in sins, and your sinful **desires** were not yet cut away. Then he gave you a **share** in the very life of **Christ**, for he forgave **all** your sins" (Colossians 2:13 TLB).

"But if we **confess** our sins to him, he can be **depended** on to forgive us and to **cleanse** us from every **wrong**" (1 John 1:9 TLB).

"Your **heavenly Father** will forgive you if you forgive those who **sin** against you; but if you refuse to **forgive** them, he will not forgive you" (Matthew 6:14,15 TLB).

```
R L G T E H E A V E N L Y S P R A T T L I R A
S E H K F J A F A J F A L A J P E R M J E S E
E S F D K E O H L P D E P E N D E D K F F L H
R L E T H E S N A E L C Y T U E O P S A E U L
I S E S N A E L C N I S O D L S A J E A E N A
S S E F N O C G O D E G N I V B C J X J D J E
E F O R G I V E E R A H S K D E E S T L L A C
D F A T H E R T S I R H C T O G N O R W B E L
```

The main point of these verses is . . .

On a separate sheet of paper write a list of sins in your life which need to be forgiven. Ask God in prayer to cleanse you from these sins. After praying, tear up the sheet of paper and throw it away, symbolizing how God forgives our sins. Then reread Matthew 6:14,15 and heed its warning.

Three-Sixteen

John 3:16 is a popular verse of Scripture. We learn a
lot about God's love for us from this verse. But there
are several other "three-sixteens" in the New Testament which teach us much about our Christian faith.
Look up each three-sixteen below and write it out
completely in the space provided.

John 3:16

1 Corinthians 3:16

Colossians 3:16

2 Timothy 3:16

1 John 3:16

Imagine that these five verses were the only passages of Scripture you had ever read. Write a paragraph below summarizing what you know about the Christian faith from these important three-sixteens.

Reaching In

In 1 Corinthians 9:19-23 Paul explains and illustrates how he was willing to do anything in order to share the gospel. Read these verses and appreciate Paul's commitment to extend himself to the various groups in his world.

In the column on the left list two groups at your school with which you are not presently associated (for example: a drama group, pep squad, party crowd). Plan a strategy for reaching those two groups and involving them in your church or youth group. Write your creative strategies on the right. If the task of reaching a new group seems difficult to you, remember Paul's words: "I can do everything through Him who gives me strength" (Philippians 4:13 NIV).

Groups to Reach   **Strategies for Reaching**

1.   A.

                              B.

                              C.

                              D.

2.   A.

                              B.

                              C.

                              D.

Wise Guys

Read Proverbs 2:1-22. List the key words which are used most often in this chapter.

1. What do you find special or interesting about these words?

2. How will these words help bring wisdom into your life?

3. Describe one situation in your life today in which you need God's wisdom. How does Proverbs 2:6 help you face that situation?

4. According to this chapter, how does a person receive wisdom?

5. Among your friends and family members, who especially needs to hear these ideas on wisdom? When will you share these thoughts with him or her?

Praise Report

Psalm 92 is a beautifully written expression of praise
to God. Read this psalm and use it as an example for
your own personal letter of praise. Take time to tell
God why you love Him. Don't ask Him for anything in
this letter. Just focus on words of thanksgiving and
praise. Keep this letter as a reminder of God's
goodness when life gets tough.

Dear God,

Personal Policy

Ask a parent to show you one of their insurance policies. Look through it and notice that the policy protects certain possessions. Each policy insures the specific possessions the policy-holder wants to protect.

Today you are the policy-holder and you get to write a policy which protects four people and/or possessions which are of great value to you. Follow the example to describe four items you want protected, why they are special to you, and what their value is to you.

Personal Insurance Policy

What I want protected	Why it is special	Its value
Cathy	She is my wife. I value our friendship, her love, and the way she makes me feel. She is the joy of my life!	Irreplaceable
1.		
2.		
3.		
4.		

Read Deuteronomy 4:31. How well-protected do you feel as God's possession?

Uh, uh, . . . Because

Read 1 Peter 3:15. If someone at school asked you why you are a Christian could you give him/her a good answer? What if they started asking questions which needed answers beyond just "faith"?

List below some questions about Christianity for which you don't have answers. Spend some time in the next few weeks trying to find answers to these questions. Ask a pastor, spend time in the church library, or consult a friend who knows more about Christianity than you do.

As you research these questions, ask God to lead you to helpful resources. Be sure to share the results of your search with a friend or family member.

Questions	Answers
1.	1.
2.	2.
3.	3.
4.	4.
5.	5.

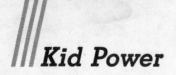

Kid Power

In Luke 9:46-48 Jesus settled a squabble among the disciples over greatness by using a child as an example. His illustration teaches us some important things about power.

Look through a newspaper or magazine and clip a few photos of some powerful people in our world. Tape these pictures on the left side of the space below. Also clip some photos of babies or young children and tape them on the right side of the space. Then answer the questions on the next page.

What are the differences between the two groups of people pictured?

What main points was Jesus illustrating when He used a small child as an example?

How would your life be different if you had more power?

Find a diaper or a diaper pin you can borrow. Place it where you will see it often over the next few days. Let it remind you of Jesus' position on power and the importance of childlikeness in His kingdom.

Marked Events

Many of Jesus' significant miracles and teachings are recorded in the Gospel of Mark. Below is a list of 16 events—one from each chapter. Search through the Gospel of Mark to discover the chapter where each is found. (It's easier than you might think!)

Circle the event that is most meaningful to you at this point in your life. Try to memorize these locations for future reference.

Event   **Chapter**

Jesus feeds the five thousand

Jesus asked, "What is the greatest commandment?"

Temptation of Jesus

Jesus casts demons out of a man and into swine

Jesus meets the rich young man

The paralytic lowered through the roof and healed

The transfiguration

The resurrection of Jesus

The last supper

Jesus talks about the end times

Jesus appoints the 12 disciples

Peter's confession of Christ

The crucifixion of Jesus

Jesus heals the Syrophoenician
woman's daughter

The triumphal entry

Jesus calms the storm

Wonder Woman

Proverbs 31:10-31 contains a thorough description of a woman who possesses godly qualities which make her shine with inner beauty. Read these verses.

If you are a female, write down five qualities from this passage which you would like to grace your life. Next to each quality write one goal that will help you develop that quality.

Female:

Qualities	Goals
1.	1.
2.	2.
3.	3.
4.	4.
5.	5.

If you are a male, write down five qualities that you would most like to see in the woman you marry. Then rank those qualities from one to five in order of their importance, number one being the most important to you. Ask God to prepare you to be the kind of man who will bring out the inner beauty in your future wife.

Male:

Qualities   **Order of Importance**

1.

2.

3.

4.

5.

Radio Waves

Listen to your favorite radio station with a pen in your hand for ten minutes straight. Write down all the themes, words, and messages you hear, both positive and negative.

Positive   **Negative**

What do you feel is positive about the music you listen to?

What do you feel is negative about your music? What do others suggest is negative about your music?

Are you aware of any controversies over Christian and/or non-Christian music in your church or community? If so, what are the issues of the controversy?

What is your opinion on the issues mentioned above?

Read Ephesians 5:19,20. What kind of music should be included in a Christian's music diet? Why?

Giving a Compass

"Dear brothers, if a Christian is overcome by some sin, you who are godly should gently and humbly help him back onto the right path, remembering that next time it might be one of you who is in the wrong" (Galatians 6:1 TLB).

Why do you think the apostle Paul stresses "gently and humbly" in this verse?

What should you do if a sinning Christian refuses your efforts to restore him/her? (Read Matthew 18:15-17.)

Do you know a faltering Christian who needs to be encouraged in his/her faith? Take some time to pray for that person. Also pray that God will help you stay on the right path.

What specific things can you do to help that faltering Christian back to the right path? List several ideas below.

1.

2.

3.

4.

5.

HEY!
— THIS WAY!

We've Got Spirit

Write a brief paragraph explaining your understanding of the Holy Spirit.

Often the role of the Holy Spirit is misunderstood and He is viewed as some type of mystical ghost or wizard who acts on behalf of God. But the Holy Spirit is a person and He has many personal characteristics we possess. Look up the following verses and make notes on what you learn about the Holy Spirit.

What are His feelings?

Romans 15:30

Ephesians 4:30

Hebrews 10:29

What are His thoughts?

    John 14:26

    Romans 8:26,27

    1 Corinthians 2:10,11

What are His desires?

    Acts 13:2

    John 16:8-11

Write another brief paragraph summarizing what you have learned about the Holy Spirit.

Comic Relief

Place the comic section of today's newspaper alongside your Bible for this session. Complete the following exercises from the two resources in front of you.

1. Look for a comic that illustrates a verse of Scripture. Cut it out, write the verse reference on it and tape it where you will see it often as a reminder.

2. Look for a comic that presents an ethical statement. Compare it to a comic presenting a message you would not endorse.

3. Cut out a cartoon that reminds you of a friend and send it to him or her with an encouraging note or Scripture verse.

4. Draw your own cartoon on a separate sheet of paper for your youth pastor. Make sure it's encouraging and amusing!

5. Illustrate a favorite Scripture verse in cartoon form. Then share it with a family member.

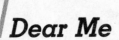

Dear Me

In Revelation 2 and 3 Jesus Christ dictated seven
letters to the apostle John to be delivered to the
churches in Ephesus, Smyrna, Pergamum, Thyatira,
Sardis, Philadelphia, and Laodicea. The letters
contained encouragement and exhortation to the
Christians in these cities. Read at least three of these
letters before continuing this exercise.

If God decided to write a letter to you today,
what would He say? Write the letter as you think
it might appear. Be sure to include both encouragement and exhortation.

Dear _____
      (your name)

I'm Thankful!

Be thankful today! You have great reason to be thankful no matter what your situation may be. Try to think of one specific reason for thanksgiving for each letter of the alphabet. It will be a challenge, but with a little thought you will be able to do it. Before you start, read 1 Thessalonians 5:18 and Ephesians 5:20.

A.   J.   S.

B.   K.   T.

C.   L.   U.

D.   M.   V.

E.   N.   W.

F.   O.   X.

G.   P.   Y.

H.   Q.   Z.

I.   R.

Making Money Count

First Timothy 6:6-10 contains wise words of warning concerning the love of money. Read these verses slowly and carefully. Evaluate where you stand in relation to the warnings presented. Could these words be speaking directly to you? Ask God to teach you something very special this week about money.

Take out a dollar bill, lay it on a separate piece of paper, and trace around it. Then divide the dollar-sized rectangle into three sections. Give each section one of the following headings: Why I like money; How money affects me; How God views money. Fill each section with your written response to the heading. Then pray that God will give you a proper perspective on money.

Christian Conflict

Read about the conflict between Paul and Barnabas in Acts 15:36-41. These servants of God were on a missionary journey planting and encouraging churches. They had a conflict, but they resolved it and continued their individual ministries with new partners.

Answer the following questions about conflicts in your life:

Is there someone in your life with whom you have had a conflict? Name the person and describe the nature of the conflict.

Have you completely resolved this conflict? If so, how did you do it? If not, what can you do *today* to help solve the problem?

Read Matthew 5:22-26 and Ephesians 4:26. What do these verses teach you about handling conflicts with others in your life?

Run Feet Run

In his letters to Timothy, Paul instructs his fellow minister to flee (run away, beat it, scram) from evil practices. Read Paul's words in 1 Timothy 6:6-11 and 2 Timothy 2:22. Then answer the following:

Why do you think Paul warns Timothy to stay away from evil practices?

What are some temptations to evil practices that Paul might warn you to flee from? List them here.

How might these evil practices affect you in the future if you don't follow Paul's advice to flee?

What are some specific ways you can flee from each of the evils you listed above?

What's Your Isaac?

God tested Abraham's faith by instructing him to present his son Isaac, whom he loved more than anything, as a human sacrifice. Read the exciting story in Genesis 22:1-18.

God wanted to see which was more important in Abraham's life—his son Isaac or his obedience to God. After Abraham proved himself, God told him, "I will surely bless you . . . because you have obeyed me" (Genesis 22:17,18 NIV).

Let's say that the "Isaacs" in our lives are those people and things which rival God for first place. List on the left below the Isaacs you are tempted to consider more important than God in your life. Explain on the right why each Isaac is or is not more important to you than God at this time.

My Isaacs are . . .   **More important than God? Why or why not?**

1.

2.

3.

4.

5.

6.

Has Jesus Gone Mad?

Read Mark 11:15-26. Then answer the following questions:

Is it difficult for you to imagine Jesus as being angry? Why or why not?

What kinds of situations would make Jesus angry today?

What makes you angry?

How do you express your anger? Do you consider your expression of anger a healthy expression? Why or why not?

What can you do this week to improve the way you deal with anger?

How can you apply this verse to your life: " 'In your anger do not sin': Do not let the sun go down while you are still angry" (Ephesians 4:26 NIV)?

Hope for a Rainbow

The biblical account of the great flood ends with God's promise which was confirmed by a rainbow in the sky. Ever since then the rainbow has been a beautiful symbol of hope. Read God's hope-filled promise in Genesis 9:8-17.

Imagine that one end of a colorful rainbow rests on your church. You have the opportunity to place the other end of the rainbow anywhere in your community which needs a ray of hope (your school, the local hangout, skid row, etc.). Where would you like to see the rainbow settle? Write your answer in the space below. Then make a list of creative ways by which you and your youth group can actually bring hope to that section of your community.

A rainbow of hope is needed at . . .

Some ideas for bringing hope to this area are . . .

1.

2.

3.

4.

5.

6.

7.

8.

Stranded on a Deserted Island

Imagine that you are stranded on a deserted island with four other people. Your basic needs for food and shelter are supplied, but you have no hope of ever leaving the island.

The others look to you as the spiritual leader even though you have no Bible. You decide to write a simple constitution to govern life on the island based on principles you remember from the Bible. Use Romans 12:18 as the goal for writing your version of a constitution below.

WHAT I SAY GOES, AND THAT'S THAT!

Old Memories

Imagine that you are 90 years old. Your eight-year-old great-grandson is cuddled in your lap. He asks you about the funniest thing that ever happened to you during your entire lifetime. You reply:

"The funniest thing that ever happened to me was . . ."

After being reminded how joyful your life has been, you comment:

"I wish I had spent less time worrying about life and more time . . ."

Then you read Matthew 6:25-34 to him and explain:

"I know I don't need to worry about life because . . ."

My Version

Select a short psalm or a collection of proverbs from the Old Testament. Write the psalm or the proverbs in your own words; make it your own unique version. Use names of people you know, locations in your community, and situations which are common to you and your age group. You will probably remember this passage of Scripture much longer because of the time you invest in trying to understand it.

Distinguished Speaker

Imagine that you are the master of ceremonies at a banquet and Jesus is the scheduled speaker. Your job is to introduce Him to the audience by telling them who He is, what He has done, and why they should listen to Him.

Write your introductory speech below. You may want to use some of the following verses to help you prepare your introduction: Matthew 1:23; John 6:51; Acts 3:15; 5:31; Galatians 3:13.

"Ladies and gentlemen, I would like to introduce Jesus Christ, who . . ."

WHAT CAN I SAY ABOUT OUR SPEAKER EXCEPT THAT... WELL... HE'S GOD.

The Master's Mail

Read 2 Corinthians 3:1-3 which describes us as living letters that can be read by those watching us. Since you are a living letter of Christ, take some time to write a letter to Him on a sheet of stationery. Explain in your letter how you are doing and why you are thankful for what He has done for you. Then tell Him what you are (or are not) doing now to display to others your love for Him.

After completing your letter, seal it in an envelope, address it to yourself and stamp it. Give the sealed envelope to a friend and ask him/her to hold it for several weeks before mailing it to you. When the letter arrives, read it again to see how you have changed over the weeks which passed.

Quality Parents

You have been chosen as the guest speaker for a national parenting conference. The assigned title for your speech is: "Qualities of a Good Parent." Your speech must include five main points. The conference group knows you are a committed Christian and they are expecting that you will use the Bible as the basis for your talk.

Outline your speech below. Include your main points and a brief example illustrating how parents can put each principle into practice. See Deuteronomy 6:4-9, Ephesians 6:4, and Colossians 3:21 for some ideas to get you started.

Qualities of a Good Parent

1.

2.

3.

4.

5.

Plan Ahead

Look back at the qualities for parenting you listed in the last session. Read those Scripture passages again and write below some specific things you can do now to prepare yourself to be a good parent.

Preparing for Parenting

1.

2.

3.

4.

5.

All parents, including yours, acquire many of their qualities from their parenting experiences. Your parents may not be perfect, but they do have some positive qualities. Write your parents a letter on a separate sheet of paper thanking them for their love and acknowledging some of their positive qualities.

Flip for Prayer

Read Colossians 1:9-12 and notice Paul's commitment to pray for others. Then grab your family address book and a coin. Flip the coin to decide who you will pray for today. If you flip "heads," turn to names beginning with A-L. For "tails," turn to names beginning with M-Z. Continue to flip the coin to narrow your choice to one name. Heads always designates the first half of the alphabet section you're working with and tails always designates the second half.

When you have selected a name, pray for that person. After praying, you may want to write a short, encouraging note saying that you have prayed for him/her.

All-Stars

Read Galatians 5:22,23 and think of the nine fruits of the Spirit as players on a team roster. From these nine select the three top all-stars you would like on your team. Write them in the appropriate spaces below.

Then write a brief, descriptive introduction of each all-star explaining why that quality is important to your team.

All-Star Number One _____:

All-Star Number Two _____:

All-Star Number Three _____:

Family Feuds

Many problems are present in homes all over the world. Conflicts occur between husbands and wives, parents and children, and brothers and sisters. Harmony in the home seems almost impossible to achieve.

List up to ten problems which occur among family members today. Next to each problem describe how you think Jesus would respond to each problem. Use Scripture references to back up your comments wherever possible.

Family problems   **How Jesus would respond**

1.

2.

3.

4.

5.

6.

7.

8.

9.

10.

Imagine that you have been invited to write a policy for peace in the homes of the world. Write your peace policy below based on what you think Jesus might write.

Poor Me

Pretend that you are a high school student in Ecuador named Juan or Juanita. Your mother and father both work to put meals on the table. You work five hours every day after school and 12 hours on the weekend to help buy supplies for your family. You must wear the same clothes to school every day because of your family's poverty.

You recently won an academic award and your government is sending you to the United States to spend a week with an American family. The family you will stay with as Juan or Juanita is your real family. You will need to adjust to the living standards and amenities which your real family enjoys. As Juan or Juanita, how do you think you will respond to your house, parents, friends, and lifestyle? Write a letter to your parents in Ecuador describing what you like and don't like about American family life. Also explain what you are learning through the experience.

Dear Mom and Dad,

The United States is not like Ecuador because . . .

Read Philippians 4:11-13. Then write a note of thanks to God for what He has given you.

International Intercession

Use a world almanac or encyclopedia to identify one specific foreign country you know little about. Gather some information about this country—per capita income, infant mortality rate, life expectancy, economic structure, etc.

Then search out information in the same categories for the United States. How do the two countries compare? What needs do you see in the foreign country you have studied?

Read 1 Timothy 2:1-4 and pray for the foreign country. Pray for its government, economy, Christians and churches, health needs, and family structures. Complete the following statements to help direct your prayers:

My foreign country is . . .

I will remember to pray for this country when I see . . .

I will pray for . . .

Mixing It Up . . . and Across

You won't find this crossword puzzle as difficult as those in the newspaper, but the answers will be more meaningful to you. Give it a try.

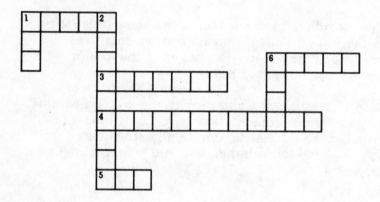

Across

1. This man is given many names and titles in the Bible.
3. "This is the _____ that has overcome the world, even our faith" (1 John 5:4 NIV).
4. According to 1 Thessalonians 5:18, we should have this in all circumstances.
5. "Therefore, if anyone is in Christ, he is a _____ creation; the old has gone, the new has come!" (2 Corinthians 5:17 NIV).
6. Jesus does this three times in Mark 5.

Down

1. The fruit of the Spirit is listed in Galatians 5:22,23. This is the only quality with three letters.
2. According to Ephesians 6:17 we are to take the helmet of _____.
6. What do we have as an anchor for the soul according to Hebrews 6:19?

Scrambled Truth

Here is a tricky one to get your mind working. Unscramble each of the words below and spell them correctly in the spaces provided. Then transfer the letter which is above each number in the verse to the corresponding numbered space in the reference below. You'll get it!

"r o f   h e t   d o r w   f o   d o G   s i
"_ _ _   _ _ _   _ _ _ _   _ _   _ _ _   _ _
          1

v i g n i l   d n a   t a c v e i ,   p a r s h e r
_ _ _ _ _ _   _ _ _   _ _ _ _ _ _ ,   _ _ _ _ _ _
15   2   4   5

n h t a   y n a   w o t - g d d e e   w o r d s ,
_ _ _ _   _ _ _   _ _ _ _ _ _ _ _   _ _ _ _ _ ,
                 6   7

r e c i i n p g   o t   h e t   s i v o n d i i
_ _ _ _ _ _ _ _   _ _   _ _ _   _ _ _ _ _ _ _ _
                                        16

o f   l o u s   d n a   p i s r i t ,   f o
_ _   _ _ _ _   _ _ _   _ _ _ _ _ _ ,   _ _
8   9

s t i o j n   d n a   r r o m a w ,   d n a
_ _ _ _ _ _   _ _ _   _ _ _ _ _ _ ,   _ _ _
                          11   13

c i d s n n i g e r   e t h   g o u t s h t h
_ _ _ _ _ _ _ _ _ _   _ _ _   _ _ _ _ _ _ _ _
                                   10

dnα   tiosnnetin   fo het

‾ ‾ ‾   ‾ ‾ ‾ ‾ ‾ ‾ ‾ ‾ ‾   ‾ ‾   ‾ ‾ ‾
          12   14

αrthe."

‾ ‾ ‾ ‾ ‾."
  17

(Note: 3 = b)

‾ ‾ ‾ ‾ ‾ ‾ ‾   ‾ ‾ ‾ ‾: ‾ ‾ ‾ ‾ ‾ ‾   (RSV)
1 2 3 4 5 6 7   8 9 10 11   12 13 14 15 16 17

Why is this verse important to you as a Christian?

Price Check

In 1 Corinthians 6, Paul talks about our physical bodies and the importance of sexual purity. Paul concludes the chapter by saying that we were "bought at a price. Therefore honor God with your body" (1 Corinthians 6:20 NIV).

How would you rate your response to this command? Put a price on the various elements of your human body between $0 and $10 based on how well they honor God. Then list what you view to be your strengths and weaknesses for each element.

Elements	Price	Strengths	Weaknesses
1. mind			
2. mouth			
3. body			
4. sexuality			
5. appearance			
6. personality			

Take time to thank God for paying the price for your life (see Romans 3:23 and 6:26) and for the unique strengths He has given you.

YOUR CREATIVE IDEA
COULD BE WORTH $100

If you have a creative devotional idea you think is worth sharing, send it to us. If we like it, we'll print it in a future devotional book, and we'll give you ten dollars and a credit line. If we select yours as the most creative idea in the book, we'll send you one hundred dollars for it.

Just send in this form with your idea. Be sure to explain the idea as clearly as possible. By the way, you can send in as many ideas as you like.

Name _____

Address _____

City _____ State _____ Zip _____

I'm submitting the attached devotional idea for possible publication in a future book on creative times with God. To my knowledge, the publication of the attached idea will not violate any copyright belonging to someone else. I understand that if my idea is published, I'll receive payment for it, the amount to be determined by the authors of the book and payable upon publication.

Signature _____ Date _____

Send to:
CREATIVE TIMES WITH GOD
P.O. Box 8329
Newport Beach, CA   92658-8329

More Books by
Doug Fields

Congratulations! You Are Gifted!
How Not to Be a Goon
Creative Dating
More Creative Dating

Other Good
Harvest House Reading

GETTING IN TOUCH WITH GOD
by *Jim Burns*

This daily devotional will take you to Scripture and provide practical application in such areas as love, prayer, the Holy Spirit, and the promises of God.

HANDLING YOUR HORMONES
by *Jim Burns*

Candid advice on how not to compromise biblical convictions when faced with difficult issues such as parties, drugs and drinking, masturbation, venereal disease, and homosexuality.

HANDLING YOUR HORMONES GROWTH GUIDE
by *Jim Burns*

A 64-page illustrated workbook with exercises and questions to help you with your own views and feelings.

HANDLING YOUR HORMONES LEADER'S GUIDE
by *Jim Burns*

Practical guidelines for creating an environment in which young people can deal openly and honestly with issues confronting them.

GOD'S DESIGN FOR CHRISTIAN DATING
by *Greg Laurie*

In the midst of conflicting worldly standards, it is still possible to find and fulfill God's design for exciting relationships with the opposite sex. Offering godly counsel with touches of humor, Greg gives the "how-to" of healthy dating.

BIBLE FUN
by *Bob Phillips*

Jam-packed full of brain-teasing crossword puzzles, intricate mazes, word jumbles, and other mind benders, *Bible Fun* will keep you occupied for hours—with the added bonus of honing your Bible knowledge.

IN SEARCH OF BIBLE TRIVIA—VOLUME 1
by *Bob Phillips*

A stimulating collection of well-known and little-known Bible facts. Don't miss this opportunity to test your Bible knowledge.

Dear Reader:

We would appreciate hearing from you regarding this Harvest House nonfiction book. It will enable us to continue to give you the best in Christian publishing.

1. What most influenced you to purchase *Creative Times with God?*
   - ☐ Author
   - ☐ Subject matter
   - ☐ Backcover copy
   - ☐ Recommendations
   - ☐ Cover/Title
   - ☐ _____

2. Where did you purchase this book?
   - ☐ Christian bookstore
   - ☐ General bookstore
   - ☐ Other
   - ☐ Grocery store
   - ☐ Department store

3. Your overall rating of this book:
   ☐ Excellent   ☐ Very good   ☐ Good   ☐ Fair   ☐ Poor

4. How likely would you be to purchase other books by this author?
   - ☐ Very likely
   - ☐ Somewhat likely
   - ☐ Not very likely
   - ☐ Not at all

5. What types of books most interest you? (check all that apply)
   - ☐ Women's Books
   - ☐ Marriage Books
   - ☐ Current Issues
   - ☐ Self Help/Psychology
   - ☐ Bible Studies
   - ☐ Fiction
   - ☐ Biographies
   - ☐ Children's Books
   - ☐ Youth Books
   - ☐ Other _____

6. Please check the box next to your age group.
   - ☐ Under 18
   - ☐ 18-24
   - ☐ 25-34
   - ☐ 35-44
   - ☐ 45-54
   - ☐ 55 and over

Mail to: Editorial Director
Harvest House Publishers
1075 Arrowsmith
Eugene, OR 97402

Name _____

Address _____

City _____ State _____ Zip _____

Thank you for helping us to help you in future publications!